THE ADV

Wipf and Stock Publishers
199 W 8th Ave, Suite 3
Eugene, OR 97401

The Advent of Justice
A Book of Meditations
By Walsh, Brian J. and Middleton, J. Richard

ISBN 13: 978-1-4982-0341-8
Publication date 8/19/2014

The Advent of Justice

A book of meditations

Brian Walsh
Richard Middleton
Mark Vander Vennen
Sylvia Keesmaat, *editor*

Illustrated by Willem Hart

WIPF & STOCK · Eugene, Oregon

Preface

The word Advent means an arrival: the arrival of a helper, a comforter, a saviour, a king and a kingdom. For Christians it has also come to characterize our waiting in the weeks leading up to the celebration of an arrival, the arrival of our God on earth in the human Jesus. These meditations are concerned with that waiting and arrival in a very specific way. Rooted in the daily lectionary readings with a primary focus on Isaiah, they contemplate God's action in history both in the eighth century B.C. and today.

The book of Isaiah has been a very rich source for reflection on God's act of salvation in Jesus. In focusing on this book in its historical setting, these meditations create in us a sense of how God might be acting through us in our time to bring healing as we anticipate the Advent of the Son once again. The New Testament passages cited are linked with the Isaiah passages in the daily lectionary; each of the authors reflects on them to varying degrees.

Just as the coming kingdom will gather in people from the four corners of the earth, so also these meditations reflect the perspectives and literary styles of four different authors. They begin the first week in Advent with Brian Walsh's dynamic analogies between Isaiah's critique of the cultures of his time and a critique of our own world. In the second week, Richard Middleton uncovers God's hand for us in the geopolitical intricacies of the text as well as in our own time. Mark Vander Vennen brings the biblical imagery to life in the third week as he unfolds an Advent which is not for the faint of heart; and in the week leading up to Christmas Sylvia Keesmaat looks forward to the ending of the story in her reflections on our current task.

These meditations are generally based on the text of the New Revised Standard Version. When a different translation is used, the author has so indicated. We would suggest that this book be used like the filling of a sandwich between two readings of the biblical text. That is to say, after you have read the texts for each day and then read the meditation, it would be helpful to read the scripture passages again on their own, either right away or later in the day. In this way, we hope, the meditations will not become a substitute for the reading of the passages on which they are based.

This little booklet has been written in joyful celebration of the thirtieth anniversary of Citizens for Public Justice (CPJ) and the CJL Foundation. We thank God for the many ways in which the work of these organizations anticipates the Advent of our God.

Sylvia Keesmaat

FIRST SUNDAY OF ADVENT

Ready or not?

Isaiah 1.1–9
Matthew 25.1–13

The ox knows its owner,
and the donkey its master's crib,
but Israel does not know,
my people do not understand.
Isaiah 1.3

Sunday

Advent is about waiting. Waiting for the Coming One. Waiting for the Messiah. Waiting in Advent, however, is not passive. The kind of waiting that we embark upon during Advent is active. The Messiah is coming, and with his coming there will be a reign of peace and justice. Therefore we must be diligent in keeping ready.

There are at least two ways that we can fail in being ready, two ways that we can "miss" Advent. The first is illustrated in the parable of the ten maidens. There is a wedding and, as is customary, the girlfriends of the bride await the bridegroom in order to accompany him to the wedding feast and celebrations. But the bridegroom is late. Middle Eastern weddings never seem to happen on time. Five of the young women anticipate this problem and come prepared with additional oil to keep their lamps lit. Five, however, are not so prepared. They do not properly anticipate the coming of the bridegroom and are not prepared in their waiting for possible delays. Five waited in readiness, five did not. Those who were ready entered the feast, those who were not ready were left outside. This is the first way to miss Advent. We can miss Advent by simply not being ready, by not living our lives in ways that constantly anticipate the coming of God's kingdom of joy, peace and justice.

But there is another way that we can miss Advent. We can miss Advent by not waiting at all. You see, if we are satisfied with our own lives, if we think that "what you see is what you get," if we have a sense that somehow we have already "arrived" and that there is no further to go, then there will be nothing to wait for. This is the reality that the prophet Isaiah faced eight centuries before Christ.

Since we will be spending a lot of time with Isaiah this Advent, let's try to sketch out his context a little. Isaiah's ministry began during the prosperous reign of King Uzziah in Jerusalem. In fact, during Uzziah's reign Judah's power and prosperity was second only to the era of David and Solomon. Although the political map was in a constant process of change (the northern kingdom of Israel fell into Assyrian captivity in 722 B.C.; the southern kingdom of Judah was busily engaging in various alliances with Egypt and Syria (Aram) in order to bolster her security over against the Assyrian threat), the mood in Jerusalem remained one of satisfied safety. After all, Jerusalem is the City of David! With the Davidic king on his throne and God in the Temple, what evil could possibly befall us? What do we have to wait for? All that we could possibly want is already here. Since we have a secure covenant with the God of Israel, we have already arrived, and the proof of that arrival is our prosperity. Who needs an Advent when the promises are already fulfilled?

Enter Isaiah with an astonishingly different reading of his times. Judah has arrived? Well, if being critically ill is your idea of arrival then yes, Judah has indeed arrived. In this opening prophecy, Isaiah cuts through the self-satisfaction of prosperity and the pretentiousness of Judah's putting trust in the covenant. He describes Judah as a body of bruises, sores and bleeding wounds. At a time when Judah understands herself to be secure in her borders, Isaiah paints a picture of aliens devouring the land and of a besieged city.

Why? Why does Isaiah see destruction and collapse where others see a secure and prosperous city? Because Isaiah knows that personal and cultural life that no longer "waits" for God's reign, because it thinks that that reign has already been realized, is in fact on a path of death. When covenantal life has been structured to serve the interests of the rich at the expense of the poor, then this is in fact a covenant with death.

The bridegroom tells the maidens, "I do not know you." Isaiah says, "Israel does not know, my people do not understand." Let us enter this Advent season with knowledge and understanding. Let us wait expectantly.

Monday

Blood or justice?

Isaiah 1.10–20
Luke 20.1–8

Even though you make many prayers
I will not listen;
your hands are full of blood.
Isaiah 1.15

There was no identity problem in Jerusalem. These people knew who they were and what they were to do. They were Yahweh's covenanted people and they knew that the way to maintain the security of covenantal life was by obeying the law. And the law was clear about their responsibility to keep sabbath and to offer sacrifices for sin, guilt and thanksgiving.

We know what it means to be God's people today, too. We go to church, pay our tithe and support the work of a variety of Christian organizations. *This* is what it means to follow Christ today.

But now comes this prophet, supposedly speaking for God, questioning us: "Who asked this from your hands?" *Who* asked this? Why, God did, that's who! Offering such sacrifices is what obedience is all about, and it is precisely because we are obedient in these matters that our security is established and our prosperity flourishes. Anyway, on what authority does this Isaiah question these divinely sanctioned practices?

Isaiah's word from the Lord leaves no doubt. "I've had enough of this burnt offering business! I can't endure any more of your hymn-sings and worship services! I hate it all! This stuff is no more than a burden to me. It's all wearing me out! In fact, you can stop your incessant prayers—I'm not listening anymore!" Why? Why have you changed your mind about what you want from us? "Because your hands are full of blood."

Yes, the Temple is an architectural wonder. Yes, we are building air-conditioned churches with large parking lots full of the latest in automobile technology. Yes, the Christian community has air time on television and radio. Yes, we can amass thousands to march for Jesus. But, into this "Christian" reality Isaiah interjects these disturbing words: "Your hands are full of blood." Could it be that in this short penetrating phrase the prophet uncovers the reality of our world, which all of our religious activities so desperately try to cover up?

Well, God, if renewed enthusiasm in our worship life and church growth isn't meeting the bill, then what is it that you really want?

Cease to do evil,
learn to do good.

But what does that really mean?

Seek justice,
rescue the oppressed,
defend the orphan
plead for the widow.

It is in such activities that covenantal people renew and maintain their identity. Indeed, the true health of a community that would live in covenant with God is gauged precisely by the way in which that community cares for those who are the weakest and most powerless. Seeking justice is not merely an interesting pastime for the politically minded among us. It is a central and indispensable sign of covenantal vitality and fidelity.

Sabbath feasts, solemn assemblies, church services and hymn-sings cannot wash the blood off our hands. Only getting our hands dirty and bloody in the seeking of justice for the oppressed can do that.

Tuesday

Idolatry or faithfulness?

Isaiah 1.21–31
Luke 20.9–19

How the faithful city
has become a whore!
Isaiah 1.2

Something has gone desperately wrong. We live in a society of unprecedented wealth yet we experience unprecedented scarcity on many levels. Double incomes somehow are not enough to keep ahead. Poverty is rising sharply in the heart of wealthy countries. We spend more on health care than any other society in history, yet disease is on the increase in the Western world. And it is becoming more and more apparent that we are engaging in a "deficit financing" with the earth that effectively robs the next generations of the creation as they should inherit it. We already feel robbed by an industrial society that has made the air unfit to breathe and the sun a major health hazard.

Yes, something has gone terribly wrong. Tenants refuse the owner of the vineyard his portion of the fruit, rejecting his servants and murdering his son. And the city of righteousness, the faithful city is now a whore!

Whenever the language of harlotry, of prostitution, is used in the scriptures, the issue is always one of idolatry. Idols are like pimps, luring the people of God away from covenantal fidelity into an illicit encounter. And such encounters always bear fruit. Bad fruit! The idolatrous harlotry of Jerusalem results in economic collapse ("your silver has become dross, your wine is mixed with water"), in political corruption ("your princes are rebels and companions of thieves"), and in social injustice ("they do not defend the orphan, and the widow's cause does not come before them"). In the same way, spiritual discernment of our present cultural malaise should seek to uncover the false gods who have failed us.

At heart, idolatry amounts to an absurd declaration of independence. In idolatry we declare our independence because we declare that we can run the affairs of our lives, including the affairs of state, economy, and society, independently of fidelity to our covenant God. Like the tenants in Jesus' parable of the vineyard, we seek to control the creation that is entrusted to us as if we had total proprietary rights. This declaration is absurd, however, because idolatry never really results in independence but in slavery. Idols require sacrifices and they are never satisfied. Such a path, says Jesus, always results in bloodshed and injustice.

But is this the way that things have to be? Are we cruelly fated to put our trust in false gods who cannot deliver on their promises? Is it inevitable that the tenants of the vineyard will abandon their stewardship and reject the owner and his representatives? Can our only response to the advent of God's son be murder? No, says Isaiah. Restoration is still possible. Jerusalem can again be called a city of righteousness, the faithful city. But such a city can only be inhabited by those who are in fact ashamed of their idolatry, who blush in the awareness that such an idolatry bears the fruit of injustice and oppression. Only those who can blush in this way are ready to receive the coming Son and give an account of their stewardship.

Wednesday

Swords or ploughshares?

Isaiah 2.1–11
Luke 20.20–26

They shall beat their swords into ploughshares,
and their spears into pruning hooks;
nation shall not lift up sword against nation,
neither shall they learn war any more.
Isaiah 2.4

If it is possible for Jerusalem to be a city of righteousness, then what would that city look like? In many ways it would look like any vibrant city, bustling with activity and full of people engaging in daily culture-building tasks. The problem is that Isaiah could see that Jerusalem was already full. It was full of the wisdom and knowledge of the world. Full of silver and gold, full of horses, chariots and other implements of military power. And, most fundamentally, Jerusalem was full of idols. This was a city that had arrived—a world class city! No wonder Isaiah perceived that the inhabitants of this city were full of pride.

It is in this context that Isaiah speaks of the advent of the day of the Lord. Rather than self-assuredly proclaiming that all is secure and life is fine as it is in Jerusalem, he speaks in the future tense. He speaks of *what will be* because it is too disheartening and too hopeless to speak only of *what is*!

Isaiah gives us a vision of a city that is indeed full, full of foreigners. But they do not come to pollute God's world with idolatrous knowledge, riches and military might. Rather, they come to be instructed in the life-giving and shalom-bearing word of the Lord.

In this vision, Isaiah goes beyond an insulated and self-enclosed spirituality of arrival and recaptures what was always Israel's mission—to be a witness and a servant to the nations. So his vision is of the word of God *going out* from Jerusalem; not remaining within the covenant community, but *going out* to minister to all peoples.

And then we come to the most startling thing in this passage: what does this word of God *do* when it goes out to the nations? It brings peace! What is startling about this is that Isaiah proclaims this vision of peace *against all of the evidence.* There was absolutely nothing in his present reality to give him any indication that such a peaceful kingdom could ever be a reality. All of the empirical (and imperial!) evidence was against him! But Isaiah's prophetic imagination is not constrained by such evidence because Isaiah's God is not limited by any empire; in fact, this God uses such empires to do his bidding.

Now notice the content of the vision. Swords will be beaten into ploughshares, and spears into pruning hooks. Precisely those tools which we use to try to manufacture and protect our own security, peace and prosperity—the tools of war and aggression—are transformed, in this vision, into implements of cultivation. Rather than destroying life in a desperate attempt to secure it, Isaiah's vision calls us to *foster* life, to open life up to new possibilities, and to be involved in cultivating creation in such a way that a just prosperity will flourish.

Thursday

Cheap grace or hopeful judgement?

Isaiah 2.12–22
Luke 20.27–40

The idols shall utterly pass away.
Isaiah 2.18

Advent. Christmas. Good news. Happy feelings. Right? So why after five days are we still hearing bad news about a day of judgement? Yesterday things were starting to look up with Isaiah's vision of nations beating their weapons of destruction into tools of cultivation. But today we are back into judgement. The Lord of hosts has a day, there is indeed an Advent. But it is a day against all that is proud and lofty, against the high mountains, against every high tower, against the ships of Tarshish. Against, against, against. Why? I want good news, not all of this negativism.

The problem is that good news without prophetic critique invariably is a cover-up. Good news that will not openly and honestly confront that which perpetuates brokenness and sin is not good news at all. An Advent without judgement isn't Advent at all. It is a secular Christmas with a store-bought peace.

Isaiah will have nothing of such a cheap grace. If the day of the Lord will be a day of justice, mercy and shalom, then it must be a day against all cultural life that fosters injustice, cruelty and war. So Isaiah lists symbols of cultural prestige—the cedars of Lebanon; places of idol worship—the oaks of Bashan, high mountains and hills; structures of autonomous security—high towers and fortified walls; and implements of economic prosperity—ships of Tarshish and beautiful crafts. Against all of this stands the day of the Lord!

And so we must discern what the day of the Lord is against in our culture. What are our symbols of cultural prestige—a BMW? Our places of idol worship—the shopping malls and the stock exchange? Our structures of autonomous security—skyscrapers and military systems? Our implements of economic prosperity—NAFTA? Do these dimensions of our cultural lives arise out of a worldview pimped by idols? If they do, then they with their idols will all utterly pass away on the terrible day of the Lord.

But is that really bad news? Is all of this *against* language really as depressing as it at first appears? Or is there a profound hope in this prophecy of a day of judgement? On that day, says the prophet, "the idols shall utterly pass away." On that day, in the face of the terror of judgement, what will people do? They will "throw away their idols of silver and their idols of gold." And as terrifying as the images of that day might be, this abandonment of idolatry is fundamentally good news. It is idolatry and the pretentiousness of life lived in the service of idols that breed despair and hopelessness.

To live with an Advent hope is to anticipate the day when the idols will pass away and we will no longer feel compelled to pay them homage. Such a hope engenders faithful living now, no longer subject to false gods of death and oppression because we are subjects of a coming kingdom of life and liberation.

Friday

Plunder or care?

Isaiah 3.1–15
Luke 20.41 – 21.4

It is you who have devoured the vineyard;
the spoil of the poor is in your houses.
Isaiah 3.14

In the Bible there seems to be a series of economic laws at work. The first law insists that economic justice can only be realized when our economic affairs are carried out as acts of stewardship for God. A second law simply states that where we see economic prosperity side by side with poverty there is always oppression involved. And a third law proclaims that where there is economic oppression social collapse is imminent. We see all three of these laws at work in today's passage from Isaiah.

Another way to describe the third law is that "the wages of sin are death" (Rom 6.23). If this is true of personal life, then it is devastatingly true of socio-cultural life as well. And so Isaiah brings a prophecy of the total collapse of the social infrastructure of Jerusalem. The supply of food and water will be cut. The military, political, juridical, religious, diplomatic and artistic institutions of society will all crumble. The result will be a social chaos in which no one will want to take the reins of leadership. But all of this has a clear cause: "Woe to them! For they have brought evil on themselves."

Yahweh rises in court to argue the case, standing to judge God's people and to give an account of why Jerusalem, the righteous city, has fallen into such chaos. Yahweh appeals to the second law: "the spoil of the poor is in your houses." You crush the face of the poor and that is why your once opulent and secure city is now in the throes of collapse! But at the root of this kind of economic oppression and the resulting socio-cultural collapse is a transgression of the first economic law. Isaiah says, "It is you who have devoured the vineyard!" Rather than making our economic decisions as stewards of a vineyard that belongs to the Creator, we have presumed to own the vineyard and to devour it as we please. Such an economic life always results in oppression and economic collapse.

Not many of us deliberately plunder the poor. But the

systems of international debt have the same effects. Since 1982, developing countries have paid more interest and principal to the wealthy countries and their banks than the total amount they received back from them in the form of investments, credits and development assistance. This means that "the spoil of the poor" is in fact in our houses! If this is true, then Isaiah's words of social collapse should have an ominous ring in our ears.

But the first economic law still calls out as an invitation. We don't have to devour the vineyard! We are still invited to a life of economic stewardship that rejoices in the call to make the earth fruitful in various ways. Such a lifestyle knows the contentedness of "enough" and the joy of an economics of care and responsibility.

Saturday

Arrival or exodus?

Isaiah 4.2–6
Luke 21.5–19

Indeed over all the glory there will be a canopy.
Isaiah 4.5

A renewed Jerusalem, a righteous branch and a new exodus. These are the images that Isaiah evokes in today's passage. Over against the contrived life that has been built up in Jerusalem, Yahweh offers an alternative.

We have seen that the economic and political realities of Jerusalem were realities formed by hands filled with blood. In this passage we hear what God ultimately wants to do with those blood-filled hands. God wants to cleanse the bloodstains of Jerusalem. Only with such a cleansing can Jerusalem again be a faithful city!

The old Jerusalem was a city rich in human pride. But the renewed Jerusalem will be a place where people are proud, not of their own accomplishments, but of the fruit of the land which they receive as a gift from the hand of Yahweh.

The old Jerusalem was secure in its covenantal pretensions. Surely the presence of God would never leave the Temple! And as long as God was in the Temple, Jerusalem could rest in its accomplishments.The people of Jerusalem would not have to wait for the Lord because they, together with their well-domesticated God, had already arrived. Isaiah's image of the presence of God in the renewed Jerusalem counteracts this self-assured sense of having *arrived* by recalling the exodus. God will be present, but not as a domesticated presence in the Temple. This God will be present in a cloud of smoke by day and a flaming fire by night. This God will be present as leader of the holy people. This must be an exodus community, on the move, a community that can wait and anticipate the day of the Lord as it walks paths of mercy and justice.

Cities, like all human cultural constructions, are for protection. The question is, where is the source of protection, and who gets protected? The old Jerusalem was carefully constructed to protect the rich and the powerful. The new Jerusalem will also be protected. There will indeed be a canopy of security over that city, a shelter from the storm. But under that canopy we will find those who had no protection under the previous system.

Isaiah can dare imagine such a renewed society because he has begun to glimpse that the day of the Lord is a day of messianic hope—the day that the *branch of the Lord* will be beautiful and glorious.

Our Advent waiting is also in the light of such a hope. We know that things are not the way they ought to be. We know that we live in a world where some have much and most have little. We know that our well-developed Western world has intentionally maintained our affluence and hidden from view those who suffer from oppression and economic want. And while Isaiah keeps insisting that we see oppression and injustice for what they are, he also offers us his prophecy of judgement in the light of a profound hope. Things do not need to be this way. But things will not change until the righteous *branch* appears. And so, in hope, we wait. What we wait for is a righteous city in which we can be at home, secure in the world. This is a city with a sheltering canopy. But even this hope is not a hope of a sense of settled arrival. Rather, this is a hope for a new exodus, for a new liberation, for a new path to walk.

Sunday

SECOND SUNDAY OF ADVENT

A harvest of disappointment

Isaiah 5.1–7
Luke 7.28–35

The Lord expected justice,
but saw bloodshed;
righteousness,
but heard a cry.
Isaiah 5.7

Today's Old Testament reading is a carefully crafted literary piece, at once a love-song, a lawsuit and an extended parable with a climactic punch line. Isaiah introduces the piece as a song for his *dodi*, a term of endearment meaning friend or beloved (v.1). Casting himself in the role of best man, he sings about his friend the bridegroom and his *vineyard*. In the ancient Near East, *vineyard*, *field* and *garden*, were common metaphors for a bride (see Song of Solomon 8.12).

Drawing the audience in to interpret the well-known metaphor, Isaiah tells how his friend the husbandman prepared the soil, planted choice vines, built a watchtower and dug a wine vat, all in expectation of a rich harvest. But this faithful preparation and care was in vain. Contrary to expectations, the vineyard yielded wild or spoiled grapes, unsuited to making wine (v.2).

Isaiah subtly connects with his hearers' patriarchal beliefs and gets their hackles up. Like the judges of the woman taken in adultery (John 7.53 – 8.11), they begin to arm themselves with the stones of righteous indignation.

Then, playing masterfully on this indignation, Isaiah executes a double switch. From playing the role of best man he now becomes groom. From singing a love-song, he moves to launching a lawsuit (vv.3-6). He invites his hearers to "judge between" him and his vineyard. Casting his hearers in the role of jury, Isaiah now ups the stakes as he initiates divorce proceedings. What more could I have done? he asks in good rhetorical style. The fault lies clearly with the vineyard. Why did it not meet my legitimate expectations?

Without waiting for an answer, he announces a drastic

course of action. If the vineyard, for all his effort, produced only wild grapes, then let it be reduced to a wilderness: unprotected, uncultivated and overgrown with briers and thorns (vv.5-6). Then, in a startling climax, he declares: "I will also command the clouds that they rain no rain upon it (v.6)!"

Up until this point, Isaiah's hearers have had no problem reading the metaphor in accordance with (admittedly harsh) cultural customs. But this last pronouncement gives them pause, for who alone can command the clouds to send or withhold rain? Certainly neither bridegroom nor farmer.

But before the shock of awareness can fully dawn upon his audience, the prophet lays his cards on the table, revealing the true meaning of the song/lawsuit/parable. The husbandman is the Lord of Hosts and Israel is God's (unfruitful) vineyard (v.7). With impeccable logic Isaiah's audience has ruled the accused guilty as charged, only to find its collective finger pointing firmly at itself. The punch line here has the force of the prophet Nathan's "Thou art the man!" addressed to King David after a similar parable in which Nathan has led David to implicate himself (2 Sam 12.7).

But the prophet has not simply *told* his listeners of Yahweh's disappointment with them. With dramatic skill he has first raised, then thwarted, their expectations for the meaning of the parable, so that they might reproduce in themselves the shock of Yahweh's disappointment. Yahweh had expected justice *(mishpat)*, but saw bloodshed *(mispah)*; had expected righteousness *(tsedeqah)*, but heard an outcry *(tse'aqah)*. With these two pairs of similar-sounding Hebrew words, Isaiah is not just making puns: he proclaims that although Israel's social life might sound like it meets God's covenantal expectations, that superficial harmony hides a basic clash of values.

In contemporary terms, we might say that God expected social justice, but found "economic growth," a superficial look-alike which seemed initially full of promise but which has produced in our time the spoiled fruit of human pain and suffering. Our single-minded pursuit of profits and "progress" (to the exclusion of the broader virtues of stewardship and compassion) may keep fooling many because it contains a grain of truth, but it ultimately disappoints the just and righteous Creator.

But God's expectations are neither self-serving like those of Isaiah's audience, nor arbitrary like those of Jesus' listeners (Luke 7.31-35). Yahweh's disappointment and the judgement to follow are rooted in a profound desire to see humans genuinely flourish. Although the vineyard will be laid waste (such are the consequences of human injustice), the Lord of the harvest has plans for a replanting—a planting which will root us in Jesus, the true vine (John 15), for our healing and for the healing of the world. Through Advent, God's righteous expectations shall ultimately bear fruit.

Monday

Discerning the times

Isaiah 5.8–17
Luke 21.20–28

Ah, you...who do not
regard the deeds of the Lord,
or see the work of his hands!
Isaiah 5.11–12

Isaiah vividly describes the "wild grapes" or spoiled fruit of Israel's social life in a series of accusations framed as "woes" (vv.8,11-12) that continue into tomorrow's reading (vv.18,20–22). The Hebrew *hoy!* can be simply an attention-getter (hey!), a pronouncement of doom (woe!) or a cry of lament (ah! or alas!), as at a funeral or other sorrowful event. In our text these are all combined.

Expressing his own cry of pained response to the violent outcry with which yesterday's reading ended, Isaiah invites us to mourn over the plight of our land. Moreover, since yesterday's reading ended with the audience implicated in the crime, standing guilty as charged, he invites us also to mourn over our own plight.

We are part and parcel of a culture which values land speculation and acquisition, two activities that displace the poor, until—contrary to the mandate to "fill the earth" (Gen 1.28)—we are "left to live alone in the midst of the land" (v.8). We are implicated likewise in a culture that thrives on hedonistic self-gratification, hungering for amusement and entertainment, rising early and lingering late to satisfy our cravings (vv.11-12). Just as Isaiah had to admit his complicity in his people's guilt and uncleanness (6.5), so it is well-nigh impossible for us to live in contemporary North America and not be deeply affected by the dominant acquisitive and hedonistic pattern of life around us.

But the tragedy is compounded by the fact that our too-full lifestyle makes us blind to the crisis of the times, with little scope to discern God's large deeds in history (v.12), especially God's "strange" or "alien" deed of judgement, as Isaiah later expresses it (28.21).

Isaiah describes this judgement as a desolation of both houses and fields, precisely the thing the wealthy have been over-acquiring. Large, beautiful houses will stand empty (v.9) and crops will fail: vineyards will yield only a gallon of wine per acre and cereal crops will produce only one-tenth of the seed required to plant them (v.10). Contrary to popular wisdom, our headlong pursuit of economic growth is ultimately unprofitable and unfruitful. Though it may appear similar to genuine justice, it yields a wasteland, unfit for human life and well-being.

Exactly how this inhuman desolation will happen is only hinted at by Isaiah. He makes brief mention of exile (v.13) or deportation, usually the result of military invasion. By this time Israel—with perhaps Judah as well—was already being annexed by Syria (Aram) to the north. The image of Sheol, the underworld, opening its mouth and swallowing both the nobility and the multitude (vv.14-17) is likely a symbolic reference to a recent major earthquake (see 2.6-22 and 5.25b). If so, Isaiah daringly discerns in these political and natural disasters the righteous and just deed of Yahweh, by which the haughty are brought low and the Lord is exalted (vv.15-16). In much the same way Jesus describes the Roman siege of Jerusalem (Luke 21.20-24), accompanied by portents in the heavens (21.25-26), as the coming judgement of God, "in fulfilment of all that is written" (21.22).

In Isaiah the result of these disasters is that the land is depopulated and lambs and goats wander untended, grazing among the desolate ruins (v.17). But our gospel text hints of a salvation beyond judgement and encourages us to raise our heads, even in this bleak landscape, in hopeful anticipation of the Advent of the Son of Man, as we discern our redemption drawing near (21.27-28).

God's alien deed

Isaiah 5.18–25
Luke 21.29–38

Therefore the anger of the Lord
was kindled against his people,
and he stretched out his hand
against them and struck them.
Isaiah 5.24

Tuesday

The woes Isaiah began describing in yesterday's reading here become broader and more sweeping, and quickly pile up in an intensifying series of abrupt accusations (vv.18,20,21,22). Alas! he cries again and again in pained acknowledgement of the people's sins. Isaiah pictures his hearers slowed down by the heavy burden of their injustice, which they drag along like a treasure they can't part with (v.18). Yet they demand immediate action from God, goading the Lord to provide a sign and so prove himself (v.19). We, of course, don't ask mockingly, but pray earnestly for God to act decisively in our historical situation to set things right (which usually means to set *our* immediate situation to rights). The irony, of course, is that it is precisely *our* calling, *our* task, to set things right (to do righteousness), if only we would cast off the ropes of injustice with which we have bound ourselves.

But we are blind to what is right, says Isaiah, confusing evil with good, darkness with light, bitter with sweet (v.20). Unaware of our blindness, we claim wisdom and shrewdness for our social ideals and policies (v.21). But our wisdom is only the expertise of self-gratification (v.22); in matters of justice we are profoundly inept, and leave suffering relentlessly in our wake (v.23). What is the root of the problem? We have rejected God's word or *torah* for our lives (v.24). Instead of submitting to the instruction of the just and righteous Creator, we have bound ourselves to our false ideals, believing we can determine for ourselves what is right.

Therefore, says the prophet, dry rot has set in to the land. Since the vineyard is unfruitful, its root and blossom are about to be consumed like tinder disappearing in flames (v.24a). Isaiah makes it clear that this destruction is no chance occurrence, but is due to the anger of Yahweh kindled against the people's injustice (v.25). This is God's ironic answer to the prayer for him to act speedily and visibly, that we may know it (v.19). Instead of the expected repetition of God's exodus deed of old, when with mighty hand and outstretched arm (Deut 4.34; 7.19; 11.2) God opened the *sea* and delivered Israel to new life, this time when God stretched out his hand the *earth* opened, in judgement, not salvation, and the mountains quaked and the corpses piled up like refuse in the streets (v.25).

But don't think it's over, says Isaiah. In ominous words he will later use as a refrain (9.12,17,21 and 10.4), the prophet declares: "For all this God's anger has not turned away, and his hand is stretched out still" (v.25). As the first sprouting of leaves indicates that a summer of riotous growth is coming (Luke 21.29-31), so Judah's early troubles will be followed (as Isaiah later makes clear) by the rise of the Assyrian empire, which will threaten the very existence of the nation in the years ahead.

In our own time we might ask what world-wide recession and structural unemployment bode for our economic future. Are they temporary malfunctions of the system or omens of worse to come? Could we be entering a period of massive judgement that "will come upon all who live on the face of the whole earth" (Luke 21.35)? Of course, we would prefer not to think such negative thoughts at Advent. But our text encourages us to face reality boldly, on guard and alert (21.34-36) to the crisis of our times.

God's cleansing fire

Isaiah 6.1–13
John 7.53 – 8.11

Now that this has touched your lips,
your guilt has departed
and your sin is blotted out.
Isaiah 6.7

Wednesday

Having described Judah as tinder-dry and ready to go up in the flames of judgement (5.24), Isaiah recounts, in vivid first-person narrative, a vision of Yahweh dominated by the image of burning. In the year of King Uzziah's death, a year that saw the Assyrian empire grow stronger and extend its imperial reach over the ancient Near East, the prophet glimpses another king, enthroned over the entire earth (vv.2-3), to whom even Assyria is subject. The Temple, where this vision takes place, functions as a window on God's throne room, but itself can contain only *the hem of his robe* (v.1)! The immensity of scale alone is staggering. But add to that the encircling *seraphim*, Yahweh's six-winged blazing heavenly attendants (*saraph* means "to burn"), whose praise of the Lord of Hosts rocks the Temple to its foundations and fills it with smoke (v.4), and Isaiah is reduced to holy and abject terror.

"Woe is me!" he cries, in solidarity with the people over whom he has just proclaimed a series of woes (5.8,11,18,20–22). In stark contrast to the scribes and Pharisees who self-righteously accuse the woman taken in adultery (John 8.4-5), Isaiah admits that all—prophet and people alike—are unclean in the presence of the thrice-holy king, the Lord of hosts (v.5).

Then, with tongs, since it is hotter than even *they* can bear, one of the seraphim takes a live coal from the brazier on the altar (v.6) and sears the prophet's lips with forgiveness and atonement, purifying him for the arduous message he is to give (v.7). Only one who knows his own sin could bring such an impossible message with integrity. Isaiah is to blind, deafen and harden the people, to confirm them in their sin, and thus in their judgement (vv.9-10). Presumably if Isaiah had known the point of the message, he would not have been so quick to volunteer (v.8). In this willingness he is perhaps unique among the prophets, for all from Moses to Jeremiah vigorously resisted their commissioning.

Isaiah's resistance is limited to a poignant question, an agonized prayer of lament: "How long, O Lord?" (v.11). To which God answers: until the devastation is complete (v.11). Until the land is depopulated through exile "and vast is its emptiness" (v.12). But the judgement will fall not just upon Ephraim, the northern kingdom. Even the "tenth" (Judah) that initially escapes devastation, will finally be burned (v.13), as if a forest fire that had by-passed a small copse of standing trees quickly turns with a change of wind to devour the last remaining patch of green. Until only a stump of that magnificent forest remains and the Lord's vineyard is reduced to rubble.

But buried deep in this thicket of radical judgement is a brief sentence of hope: "The holy seed is its stump" (v.13). These cryptic words which close the vision, and the chapter, draw on the image of burning as purification (1.25; 4.3-4; 6.6-7). They also evoke the regenerative power of felled trees, especially oaks and terebinths, which in scripture are often associated with holy places and sacred groves (Gen 12.6; 35.4; Deut 11.30; Josh 24.26; Judg 9.6,37; Hos 4.13; Ezek 6.13). But beyond these associations, the text anticipates Isaiah's messianic image in 11.1 (also 11.10 and 4.2) of a branch or shoot sprouting from the stump of Jesse (the Davidic line). In a bleak text, dominated by judgement, which realistically faces the fact of national destruction, we find tucked away a hopeful hint of the advent of a future king, born by God's gracious purging of the Davidic line, to bring justice, healing and holiness, finally, to the devastated land.

Thursday

Faith and politics in Advent

Isaiah 7.1–9
Luke 22.1–13

If you do not stand firm in faith,
you shall not stand at all.
Isaiah 7.9

The background to the events of Isaiah 7-12 is an important political crisis, described concisely in Isaiah 7.1 (see also 2 Kings 16.5-9). While Judah had for many years pursued a policy of non-resistance as a vassal state to the encroaching Assyrian empire, many anti-Assyrian alliances sprang up throughout the region. One such was led by Rezin, king of Syria (Aram), who was joined by Pekah, newly ascended to the throne in Ephraim, the northern kingdom. Together these kings and their armies marched against Judah in 734 B.C., seeking to lay siege to Jerusalem and replace King Ahaz with a puppet who would willingly join the anti-Assyrian coalition (v.6). Ahaz was understandably shaken (v.2).

But his fear was not limited to these external threats. Judah had already suffered so much at the hands of its Assyrian overlords and previous military raids from Syria that Ahaz's popularity (and his pro-Assyrian policy) was at an all-time low. Like the chief priests and scribes of Luke 22.2, he lived in fear of his own people. He needed no Gallup poll to know that he faced the threat of an internal coup. In this highly charged context God sends Isaiah with a message of encouragement and warning.

On the one hand, God assures Ahaz that the Syro-Ephraimite plot against Jerusalem will come to nothing (v.7), since these kings even in their "fierce anger" are only "two smouldering stumps of firebrands" (v.4) soon to be extinguished by the Lord of Hosts. Isaiah thus encourages Ahaz not to be afraid, but to remain firm in his political resolve not to join the anti-Assyrian coalition (v.4).

On the other hand God's protection of Jerusalem is by no means unconditional. "If you do not stand firm in faith, you shall not stand at all," Isaiah announces, both making a pun (which the English tries to reproduce) and alluding to God's ancient promise (2 Sam 7.16) that David's kingdom would *stand* or *be made firm* forever (the same verb is used). But Isaiah distinguishes this promise from cheap grace by placing significant responsibility for the political future squarely on the shoulders of Ahaz and his companions (the *you* in v.9 is plural). Ahaz is challenged to remain steadfast in faith if God is to protect Jerusalem and the Davidic dynasty.

As it turns out, Ahaz's faith was ambiguous (see 2 Kings 16.7-18 for details). Although he did resist the Syro- Ephraimite coalition, he is judged ultimately to be an evil, idolatrous ruler who did not do what was right in the eyes of Yahweh (2 Kings 16.2-4).

Though Isaiah 7 is less clear in its judgement, an important hint may be discerned in the introductory notice that the prophet inconveniently had to *go to* the king to deliver his message. Ahaz was at "the end of the conduit of the upper pool on the highway to the Fuller's field" (v.3), a location outside the city walls (see 36.2 and 2 Kings 18.17), inspecting the water supply and fortifications in anxious anticipation of the coming siege. The contrast with his son Hezekiah is clear to anyone who reads ahead in Isaiah: in response to the later, Assyrian siege of Jerusalem (701 B.C.), Hezekiah actively sought out Yahweh in the Temple to pray for help and received God's blessing and assurance of protection (37.1,14-35). Isaiah 7, however, does not resolve the question of Ahaz's faith; it simply poses it. Isaiah's message to King Ahaz thus addresses us in our contemporary crises, challenging us beyond a cheap, sentimental celebration of Advent, to a faith that indeed makes a *political* difference.

Friday

Coming to terms with change

Isaiah 7.10–25
Luke 22.14–30

The Lord will bring on you
and on your people and on your ancestral house
such days as have not come
since the day that Ephraim departed from Judah
—the king of Assyria.
Isaiah 7.17

The ambiguity of Ahaz's faith, hinted at yesterday, becomes an issue in today's Isaiah text. When offered a sign as confirmation of God's promise to protect Jerusalem (v.11), Ahaz refuses under the pious guise of not wanting to "test" God (v.12). This surface piety, however, disguises a deeper fear of risk, indicating that Ahaz's pro-Assyrian policy was less a matter of trust in God than of political caution. For this timidity, Isaiah accuses Ahaz of testing or wearying God (v.13).

A sign is given to the faithless king, nevertheless. The young woman (the article is definite, indicating the queen or some Davidic princess) shall conceive and bear a son (v.14), a potential heir to the throne, to continue the royal line God promised to establish.

While the birth of an heir is already a sign of hope, the child's name, *Immanu-el* ("God with us"), heightens that hope. In addition, a time-frame for fulfilment is given. Before the child is weaned from baby food and knows how to discern right from wrong, the threat to Judah will have dissipated (vv.15-16).

But just as we want to celebrate the coming of this promised heir, Isaiah's oracle switches abruptly from assurance to threat (vv.17-25). In words that foreshadow his subsequent prophecies, Isaiah indicates that the coming of the king of Assyria signals a *new epoch* for Israel, the coming day of Yahweh (vv.18,20,21,23) as significant as the division of the kingdom in the tenth century (v.17). Just as the departure of Ephraim from Judah signalled the end of the united monarchy, so the coming of the Assyrian empire signals the end of Judah's independence and of the political aspirations of the Davidic line.

Henceforth the people of God will have to come to

terms not just with reduced ambitions, but with the wholesale devastation portrayed in verses 18 to 25. What role is there for a royal house and a holy city in an epoch of foreign invasion and occupation (vv.18-19), in a time of humiliation and defeat (vv.20-25)? What indeed could *God* have in mind, especially since Isaiah makes it clear that this epoch of judgement is God's own doing (v.17)? How can this same God reaffirm the promises of protection for Jerusalem and the house of David and, in the same breath, decree marginality and suffering for the people?

Perhaps we who live after the birth of Christ and celebrate his Advent can glimpse in Isaiah 7 the ultimate purpose and culmination of God's protection of the Davidic line: the coming of a king who suffers for the sins of his people, to deliver them not just from political plots or the bondage of empires, but from the imperial captivity of sin and death. "Immanuel" is indeed an apt description of God's incarnate presence in Jesus, who came among us to restore justice and shalom to all creation, including our social and political lives.

Yet we, too, live in the tension between the fullness revealed in Jesus and the grim realities of political fragmentation, economic recession, and mandatory "social contract" cuts. Where is God in this scene? Is it possible for us to discern the signs of the times, as Isaiah did two and a half millennia ago? Can we claim the hand of God at work in our world, both bringing judgement for our culture's accumulated injustices and constraining us to live under the sign of the crucified Messiah? Can we avoid both triumphalism and despair and walk in bold faith instead? Or is that just *too* bold? Perhaps, like Ahaz, we prefer to play it safe and not test God.

Saturday

Faithful living in an age of panic

Isaiah 8.1–15
Luke 22.31–38

But the Lord of Hosts,
him you shall regard as holy;
let him be your fear,
and let him be your dread.
Isaiah 8.13

Deliverance and judgement intermingled continue to characterize our Isaiah text. While Jerusalem is under seige, God tells Isaiah to write on a large clay tablet, "The spoil speeds, the prey hastens" (Hebrew: *maher-shalal-hash-baz*) as a witness to the coming deliverance. Then, somewhat later, but before the siege is lifted, Isaiah's wife (the *prophetess*) bears a child who is to be named *Maher-shalal-hash-baz*, the same peculiar words as on the tablet (v.3). Like Immanuel, this name is a sign of hope, clearly specifying the doom of Judah's enemies. And as with Immanuel, a time-frame is given. Before the child says its first words ("Daddy" or "Mommy"), the wealth of Syria (Aram) and Ephraim will be carried off as spoil by the Assyrian king (v.4).

Yet Judah is spared one enemy only to be almost drowned by another. Since the people are opposed to Ahaz's policy of submission to Assyria (characterized as *the waters of Shiloah that flow gently*, v.6), God is bringing *the mighty flood waters of the River*, symbolizing the Assyrian king (v.7). The *river* of Assyria will not just flood Ephraim and Syria, it will overflow into Judah and *reach up to the neck* (v.8). Isaiah hints that only Jerusalem, which is the *head* of Judah (see 7.8), will be spared, a thought that leads him to challenge Jerusalem's enemies to do their worst since it will be thwarted by the gracious presence of "God with us" (vv.9-10).

Isaiah then receives a stern warning from God (perhaps in response to his outburst of confidence) not to be fooled by the false bravado of the people (v.11). Rather than being carried away by the general panic of the times, Isaiah is to be in holy awe of the Lord of hosts who is the real actor in the momentous political drama being played out here (v.13). Although this God will be a sanctuary of refuge for those who trust in his historical purposes (difficult though they are to accept), for the majority who want to resist the Assyrian empire (as was appropriate in the past) God will become a stone of stumbling and a rock of offense (v.14).

Just try telling Jews in the eighth century B.C. (or modern Christians in the twentieth A.D.) that the good old days of glory and triumph are over and that God now wills judgement and suffering for the nation's massive sins, a suffering which can still be minimized, but not averted, if only they follow a policy of non-resistance. Changed times require a changed discernment, and Isaiah has been trying to prepare Judah for its drastically transformed role in the world. But to no avail. Even Jerusalem will resist (v.14), God grimly predicts, and many will stumble and fall, be snared and captured (v.15).

In our own period of chaos and panic over free trade agreements, factory closings, and government budget cuts, how do we find our orientation? It is easy to be swept away—almost drowned—by the wave of fear that sustains public reaction to events beyond our control, especially when that fear fuels a holy impatience born of biblical sensitivities. Yet if Isaiah's discernment applies at all to our turbulent, recessionary times, so does his challenge to a quiet, persevering trust in God. Such trust, explains Peter (quoting Isaiah 8.12-13), is a fundamental prerequisite for our witness to the gospel—*even if it leads to our suffering* (1 Pet 3.14-17). In this we will simply be following our Lord, whose Advent in likewise turbulent times was, after all, the beginning of his journey to the cross.

Sunday

THIRD SUNDAY OF ADVENT

The world court

Isaiah 13.6–13
John 3.22–30

I will put an end to the arrogance of
the haughty and will humble the pride
of the ruthless.
Isaiah 13.11 (NIV)

We now enter the third week of Advent. Like Lent, Advent is dark, intense, tumultuous as it moves forward, until that climactic burst of light in the Advent of God. Our readings from Isaiah have reflected this heightened agitation, as if in Advent the ground is now shifting like a California earthquake under our feet; as if suddenly the contractions of childbirth are coming on rapidly now, one on top of the other.

And well these readings should reflect agitation. For the birth of the child Immanuel—an exhilaration which lies at the heart of Isaiah, the gospels, ourselves—also sets in motion an accusation. Indeed, the birth of Immanuel begins legal proceedings in the court of world history, in which the Holy Spirit acts as counsellor against the prince of chaos, violence and death (John 16.7-11). Unlike the courts as experienced by many today, this court brings justice, healing, surprise and shalom.

This "world court" metaphor is the context of Isaiah (cf. Isa 3.13). The remarkable mystery is that Isaiah is given a vision of the proceedings in their entirety, from the beginning of world history to its end, as they unfold in the events of his own time! He views the events of his day from the inside out—from the perspective of heaven, earth's throne room, not solely from the surfaces which earth provides. In heaven "a day is as a thousand years," and the Messiah, though born in the middle of history, is the Beginning and End, the One who is, was, and is to come.

The birth of the Messiah thus sets in motion an accusation, which, here paraphrased, forms the backdrop to today's Isaiah passage: "I cared for you intently as my own daughter. Yet you have rejected your lineage (Isa

1.2-3), refusing to practice justice and righteousness and a sabbatical economic rhythm. You have refused to preach good news to the poor, to bind up the brokenhearted, to free the captives, to release the prisoners (Isa 1.15-17). Had you done so—an easy yoke and a light burden—I would have made your land fertile and secured it (Isa 1.19-20). But because you have become oppressors yourselves, I will send Assyria to oppress you, to take you captive and make you slaves (Isa 8.1-10)—until you learn the way of blessing."

In today's text, Isaiah is transported several decades further into the future and sees that God will also *judge* Assyria for this act. And as our eyes scan this startling funeral dirge about the city of Babylon, which Assyria had recently captured, they tumble on the verse cited above today's meditation, and remain there for a moment.

A persistent, stubborn question emerges: Why *should* God put an end to the arrogance of the haughty and the pride of the ruthless? In the face of the unending failures of humankind, also today, *why shouldn't God just let the haughty and ruthless carry on?* What prompts God to humble the arrogance of the ruthless?

Ah...wait. Let us avoid the trap of filling in the pause which follows this question, this pregnant pause, with a quick answer. Let us hold on to the question instead. This week let us lift up this question without immediately answering it; let us approach it, study it, experience it, turn it over, dissect it. Why should God end the arrogance of the ruthless?

It is clear that God *does*. For look! There is John the Baptist! In the mysterious timing of heaven in relationship to earth, the legal battle is both proceeding and already determined! Though the judgement has not yet been finalized, the outcome of the judgement is already unfolding! See, John is making clear a pathway in the desert and on it moves a motley, glorious procession of freed captives, met by a bridegroom as if on a wedding march, returning from exile, coming home to the promised land of healing, shalom! And to make room for the procession—as Moses did for Joshua, David for Solomon, Elijah for Elisha—John must now stand aside.

Let the procession begin!

Monday

Wake-up call

Isaiah 8.16 – 9.1
Luke 22.39–53

[Why do you consult] mediums and
spiritists, who chirp and mutter?
To the law and the testimony!
Isaiah 8.19a, 20a
(author's translation)

In the pedagogy of the desert, God had stripped the Israelites of the practices of Egypt and imprinted upon them the law of life, the way of blessing. The practices of Egypt and the surrounding nations had at their centre mediums, spiritists, magic, idol worship. We need to clear away the underbrush of our time to see that to them these practices were not bizarre but entirely rational and logical. They made perfect, logical sense, for they gave access to the forces of nature, which were the source of their economic prosperity. And Egypt was the wealthiest, most successful nation of its day!

On the surface, that is. For how ironic it is that in today's passage Isaiah is shown that such practices bring different results: no light of dawn, God withdrawn from the land, hunger, people thrust into thick darkness! Turn to the law and the testimony instead, says Isaiah!

It is a tragic deception of our time that rationality has come to mean the opposite of magic and idol worship. For are they not two sides of the same coin as much today as in the ancient world? Our economy is a purely rational structure, yet without a mysterious "invisible hand" working frenetically at its very centre it could not operate. Against a rising mountain of evidence, our society still stubbornly holds to the belief that an invisible hand will somehow ensure not only that the poor will participate in the rising wealth but also that natural resources will never run out and that employment will keep increasing. As Al Gore writes, "It is almost as if the ultrarational 'economic man' of classical theory actually believes in magic."

Others speak of the technological "sleepwalk" of our time. They argue that today's stunning new technologies —crowning achievements of reason, rationality, logic— could not exist without a mesmerizing sleep condition, by which we accept *without question* the rapid pace of technological change. They also argue that this sleep is central to how we experience a very familiar piece of electronic technology: television. Thousands of flickering cathode rays assault our vision in frenetic, rapid-fire succession, 32 frames per second, every day. With incantations of light, the chirping and muttering is hypnotic in effect; we are entranced, drugged.

Perhaps our sleep is like that of the disciples in Luke 22, who slept through possibly the most momentous point of history. Inattention is the opposite of love. But Jesus issues a jolting wake-up call: *precisely* in the hour when darkness reigns (v.53), Jesus *heals* his enemy (v.51), the very one who has come to thrust him into thick darkness. It is crucial for us to see that this act is not an aberration but lies at the heart of the meaning of Advent.

This Advent, what healing steps might we take out of our induced magic sleep and the sleep of our time?

Tuesday

Slivers of light

Isaiah 9.1–7
Luke 22.54–69

For unto us a child is
born...and his name shall be
called Wonderful Counsellor...and
the government shall be
upon his shoulders.
(Handel's *Messiah*)

After the darkness, cursing and hunger of yesterday, our passage today reads like sudden rest, like a quiet eddy in the often stormy river of Isaiah. How exhilarating, these words!

Isaiah, like other Old Testament prophets, links the name *Wonderful Counsellor* with *king*. Who then will be this king? And what will be his royal program?

His throne will be founded on *justice* and *righteousness* (v.7), not fertility and cult, the foundations of Baal's throne. For Israel, justice and righteousness included practising, in perfect freedom, a regular economic rhythm of cancelling debts, letting slaves and prisoners free (which diminished one's workforce), returning bought land at no cost to its original owners, letting land rest. The economics of care prescribed by the *Jubilee* legislation (Deut 15; Lev 25) made it impossible to accumulate wealth without interruption. It was an economics of *blessing*, where all that was weak, like a newborn child in the midst of a quarrelsome adult world, was brought from the margins to the centre, for the sake of justice, neighbourliness, healing, shalom. If followed, there would be no poor among them (Deut 15.4). If the economic doctrine of the surrounding nations was, "when we have accumulated wealth, *then* it is possible to share with the poor," then the biblical notion of economics was, "if we share with the poor *before* we have accumulated wealth, then we will become wealthy." Will this also hold for the newborn king?

He will also be the *Prince of Peace*, making all the warriors' boots kindling for the fire (v.5)! Will this too fall into Israel's broader military rules, including God's ban on the purchase of horses and chariots—the most advanced weapons of the day, used by the tens of thousands against

Israel (Isa 2.7; cf. Deut 17.16-17; 20.1; 1 Kings 10.26-29; Isa 31.1-3; Mic 1.14; 5.10-15)?

And then we scan forward and we see that the Jubilee theme is so central in Isaiah and the gospel that Jesus, in his inaugural sermon, adopts its fulfilment as his mandate on earth (Isa 61.1-2, Luke 4.16-21; cf. Zech 9.9-10, Luke 19.35-44). This king, it seems, with his Advent, will confirm and *vindicate* Jubilee justice and righteousness for all time (Isa 9.7)!

But as we take it in, suddenly we come up short: All of this is foolish, irrational, illogical—*nonsense in every way*! It contradicts the received economic and military wisdom, no less today than in the ancient world. How can you have an economy today without a full-fledged credit system, for example? Isn't this impossible?

Perhaps then the relief of our text is not really so welcome after all. Maybe, like Peter, we discover that the Christ-child brings to our darkness slivers of light—illuminating, yes, but poignant, even painful. Perhaps this particular Advent it will not be so easy, should not be so easy, to sing along with this chorus of Handel's *Messiah*.

Wednesday

The action of light

Isaiah 9.8–17
Mark 1.1–8

John ate locusts and wild honey.
John 1.6

Today, Isaiah is made privy to a dialogue unfolding in the court of world history. He listens in on a back-and-forth debate between God and Israel (the northern kingdom), interspersed with executions of judgement from the court. He then records these proceedings as a single poetic section of stark images, bounded by a refrain repeated four times (Isa 9.8 – 10.4).

To begin, a word came to Israel, says Isaiah (v.8): a light in the darkness, a bar of oppression broken, a Prince of Peace coming, justice and righteousness established, a Jubilee economic rhythm of care vindicated (Isa 9.1-7).

Israel's response: "*all the people knew it*...but in pride and arrogance of heart they said, `The bricks have fallen, but we will build with dressed stones; the sycamores have been cut down, but we will put cedars in their place'" (v.9-10)! Faced with the light, the Israelites choose the route of the other nations and redouble their efforts at self-aggrandizement and ambition. The Israelites could build such stone mansions using materials once reserved solely for Solomon's palace (1 Kings 7.7,9) only if they trampled on the poor and took from them levies of grain (Amos 5.11).

Then comes anger, God's overwhelming anger. "For all this his anger has not turned away; his hand is stretched out still" (v.17).

How are we to understand this seemingly inexplicable decision by the Israelites? Let us recall the action of light: light both illuminates and blinds. If we are faint of heart, the sheer brightness of God's light may overwhelm us until we turn away, unable to face it. Then, for example, we build an ambitious scenario which requires the poor to be trampled over, in which wealth and poverty circle but never find each other. Or we push out of economics all issues of caring for one's neighbour, finding them too much to even contemplate, leaving instead a pure, neutral, logical system of interest rates, money supply, inflation, prices—as if economic life were a mechanism of gears, sprockets, levers, pump-priming.

But these are acts of cowardice. Perhaps, in a negative way, they are also indications of just how blindingly bright the light is.

In any event, there again is John the Baptizer standing resolutely in the blinding light of the desert. In the desert, wild John is preaching poverty of spirit, a baptism of repentance, the stripping away of self-reliance and of the material props of our lives. He wears only rags laced together with the scant material found in the desert, and for food he depends solely on what little the desert supplies: locusts and wild honey.

No one can come to the Messiah without going through the pedagogy of the desert, the pedagogy of John.

Thursday

Not for the faint of heart

Isaiah 9.8 – 10.4
Matthew 3.1–12

They devoured the flesh of their own kindred.
Isaiah 9.20

Daniel Berrigan, one of the most prophetic Christians of our time, has spoken, in reference to today's text, of our *cannibal culture*: brother consuming brother, might going up against might. It was this which left its imprint on Berrigan: "They gorged on the right, but were still hungry, and they devoured on the left, *but were not satisfied*; they devoured the flesh of their own kindred" (v.20).

Our cannibal culture: bloodshed in Bosnia, Iraq, South Africa, Liberia, Somalia, Lebanon, Sri Lanka; industries producing poisonous DDT for export to the Third World, weapons of unfathomable destruction. Why is it that our desire for the flesh of our own sisters and brothers seems so entirely insatiable?

Today's text speaks in a graphic, revolting image. No romantic imagery, this: it is direct, quick and strong. It thus provides literary support for our lesson of yesterday: Advent is not for the faint or frail of heart but for the courageous, for those who have been given courage. The faint of heart (cf. Isa 1.5), while knowing the word of God, and in the face of the light, "write oppressive statutes, [which] turn aside the needy from justice and...rob the poor..." (10.1-2). Says God to these people of power, "To whom will you flee for help, and where will you leave your wealth?" (10.3). But those with courage write statutes and laws in the understanding that each member of a particular community, no matter how weak, is *essential*, and must be fully honoured in the writing.

The counterpoint to today's cannibal imagery, of course, is the Messiah, who emptied himself, took on the form of a servant, and gave his body and blood as sustenance so that we might have life. Servanthood is the courageous act of giving oneself to one's neighbour, one's brother and sister, both personally and in society's social, economic and political patterns. This, says Jesus, is the easiest of all yokes, the lightest of all burdens!
How utterly, gloriously different than the cannibal cultures of Isaiah's day and ours!"

Indeed, Advent reveals a startling truth: those who, in the name of the newborn king, seek first the good of the other, will be given enough and then some; but those who pursue self-interest will in the process *consume the other and never be satisfied.*

Friday

Working along the grain

Isaiah 10.5–27
Matthew 11.2–15

The remnant of the trees of his forest will be so few that a child can write them down.
Isaiah 10.19

Assyria is coming! On behalf of those on the margins, God begins to permit Assyria to take Israel into captivity. God intervenes on behalf of those whom Israel, though seeing the light, chose to trample over. One way or another, God succeeds: either through blessing or curse, the poor are protected, and the land is given its rest.

Even in this act, however, Assyria is guilty; haughty and ruthless Assyria, though she is the rod of God's hand, is no better than Israel! "This is not what he intends," wails God, as if stunned, "it is in his heart to destroy"! (v.7). Thus the fire of God will rage against Assyria, burning so completely that, "the remnant of the trees of his forest will be so few that *a child can write them down.*"

Yet even when all seems lost, a tiny, almost invisible light shines, a light which the thick black darkness cannot actually overpower: a remnant of captives shall return to God from exile! says Isaiah (v.21). A remnant which, thanks to the action of God, will finally understand that a right relationship with God and with neighbour includes practising justice, righteousness, and a Jubilee economic rhythm of care!

And there again is John, in prison now, near the end of his time, with a final question: Are you the One who will bring the captives back from exile? Jesus replies: "Go and tell John what you hear and see: the blind receive their sight, the lame walk, the lepers are cleansed, the deaf hear, the dead are raised, and the poor have good news brought to them" (Matt 11.4-5)! See, justice, righteousness and the Jubilee rhythm of relationship with others are now being vindicated! So the case, for John and all of the prophets, is closed at last.

Jesus' life, like Advent, should not be read as an abstract agenda. No, both Jesus' life and Advent are more concrete. They are more direct and immediate. They touch all; they grapple with us at our depths urging each generation to discern their relevance anew.

Both Jesus' life and Advent provide an unmistakable political and economic *direction*; they reveal a grain as clear as the grain of oak or cherry. It is a grain so entirely obvious that *even a child,* alert to the promptings of God, *can make it out.*

Saturday

Alleluia!

Isaiah 42.1–12
John 3.16–21

He will not grow faint or be crushed until he has established justice in the earth.
Isaiah 42.4

Suddenly now, in the first of four of Isaiah's Servant Songs, the tone has changed. The shifting, careening plates of rock under our feet have fallen into place. The tortuous labour appears finished, resolution is coming! What a joyous, mature, supple, marvellous text! "Sing to the Lord a new song, his praise from the end of the earth!" (v.10).

Perhaps now, with these passages, we begin to catch a breathtaking glimpse of an answer to the question we raised at the beginning of this week: Why shouldn't God just let the haughty and ruthless carry on? Given our unending failures, why shouldn't chaos, violence and death have their way? Today's passages settle on an answer something like this: Because all that God has made is still good. It is worth saving. If the haughty and the ruthless were permitted to carry on, then they would undo God's ongoing act of *blessing* humanity and all of life (Gen 1.22; 8.22 – 9.1; Exod 1.7). If the inattention, the magic, the sleep of our time and indeed of all the ages, were permitted to gain the upper hand, they would bring chaos and ruin; they would dismantle God's stunning handiwork. They would obstruct God's desire to have the creation be the blessing that God intends it to be! This is why God chooses to humble the haughty and ruthless.

As citizens in pursuit of public justice, this too forms the source of our passion. God did not send his Son into the cosmos to condemn it, but to save it through him. The world court exists for *blessing*, not for condemnation.

And so it is that all of creation, from every corner, bursts into exuberant song—from the sea and all that is in it, to the coastal lands and their inhabitants, the desert and its towns, the villages and their inhabitants, all the way to the tops of the mountains (v.10-12)! Creation sings because the *weakest* have been protected: the eyes of the blind are opened, the prisoners are released (v.7), the bruised reed miraculously survives, the candle's dying flame does not get blown out (v.3). In the economy of the kingdom, the practice of justice and righteousness are intimately linked to the fertility and inhabitability of the creation. The creation is finely attuned to the ways of God.

In the end, all of God's people will be led, as if in a new exodus, out of Assyria, Babylon, Rome; out of unjust, skewed family, economic and political relationships; out of the dark shadows and into the light; out of the burning heat of all of this and into the cool shade of the trees. Then the song on everyone's tongue will be: Alleluia!

Advent, the coming of God to dwell among us: Alleluia!

Sunday

FOURTH SUNDAY OF ADVENT

A healing kingdom

Isaiah 11.1–9
Revelation 20.1–10
John 5.30–47

They will not hurt or destroy
on all my holy mountain;
for the earth will be full of the knowledge of the Lord
as the waters cover the sea.
Isaiah 11.9

The kingship and lordship of Jesus. The central confession of Christians in the first century and the central confession of Christians worldwide today. The vision of the coming rule and kingdom of Jesus the Messiah forms the climax of the Revelation to John; our reading of the Bible finishes with John's vivid picture of the kingdom which we await.

Our anticipation of that kingdom has been our focus throughout Advent. And as part of that anticipation we have been exploring together how our current situation does or does not live up to that kingdom. Like Isaiah critically engaging his own situation, we have been critically assessing our context, acknowledging our guilt even as we hope for healing.

In this last week of Advent our focus shifts somewhat from the assessment of our own complicity in injustice to the vision of the future kingdom we await. We look forward, not so that we might forget our current needs and failures, but so that we may put our own situation in context. Knowing what our God has in store for us creates a context in which we may truly live in ways which bring the healing and the justice which God intends.

But what exactly is that kingdom all about? Again and again at Christmas we hear the rousing words of Handel's *Messiah*: "And He will reign for ever and ever!" These are words that look forward to the coming reign of Christ, to the establishment of the kingdom of God on earth. But what do these words mean? What will the reign of Christ look like? How will it affect life on this earth?

We can get some idea of the answer to this question

from Jesus himself, from the sort of kingdom he inaugurated when he was on this earth. Jesus himself tells us: my Father has given me certain work to finish, and it is this work which shows that I am from the Father; this work reveals what kind of king God really is. In the works of the Son we can catch a glimpse of what the kingdom is all about.

Well, what were those works?

The gospels are full of them: Jesus healed the sick, he forgave sins, he cast out demons, he welcomed those who were on the fringes of society, he fed people who were hungry, he calmed a threatening storm, he even brought to life those who were dead. Jesus demonstrated how the reign of God would affect the whole of creation: nature would no longer be a threat; there would be food for plenty; those normally outcast would again be welcomed in society; there would be no more sickness; there would be no more death.

In fact, says Jesus in John, these are the sorts of works which the Old Testament witnesses to; by reading the Old Testament you can assess whether I truly am bringing the kingdom of the Father. It is very possible that Jesus had a text like Isaiah 11 in mind as he said this. Jesus, on whom the Spirit of the Lord rested, also reflected in his actions Isaiah's hope for the kingdom. His ministry was an example of how one judges with righteousness, how one decides with equity for the poor of the earth. He showed what it is to have the spirit of knowledge and fear of the Lord, what it is to have wisdom and understanding. His ministry showed how the created order would exist in harmony, how life could be lived so that healing and righteousness triumph over hurt and destruction. In Jesus we see what it means to truly delight in the fear of the Lord, to truly live as though God were king.

Do we who have the knowledge of the Lord today, envisage this sort of a kingdom? For if we do, that should be evident in the works we do as well: in the ways that we righteously deal with the poor, the way that we work for creational harmony, the way that we draw in the outcast in faithfulness, the way that we bring healing rather than destruction to our current situations. For in doing these works, we too proclaim the work of our Father, and announce the nature of the kingdom for which we wait.

Monday

A sign for the nations

Isaiah 11.10–16
Revelation 20.11 – 21.8
Luke 1.5–25

He will raise a signal for the nations,
and will assemble the outcasts of Israel,
and gather the dispersed of Judah.
Isaiah 11.12

The exodus was the most powerful experience Israel had of her God. For in the exodus God had heard the people groaning in a strange land and had led them out of that land, through the waters of the Red Sea, through the wilderness and back to the land which had been promised to Abraham, Isaac and Jacob. Today we read that God's future action of salvation would be like the first: in these verses Isaiah describes salvation in terms of a new exodus. The great and glorious kingdom which we considered yesterday will be the result once more of an exodus event, an event where God gathers in his people.

But the situation is slightly different this time around. Israel is not in slavery in Egypt—she is under judgement, awaiting exile, soon to be scattered over the world. This is a prophecy of hope in the thick of judgement, a hope when despair seems to have won. In the face of a sentence that will send the people of Israel to many countries, Isaiah looks to a time beyond judgement when God will gather the people from all of the various places they are scattered, from the four corners of the earth.

And once they are restored, the people of God will once again be able to fulfil their calling: they and their Messiah will be a signal to the nations. They will be a sign of their glorious God; so much so that the nations will come to inquire after this God, the nations will come to see what God this is who can do such glorious things.

In John the Baptist, this worldwide gathering of the people of God began to take place. John would be the one to "turn many of the people of Israel to the Lord their God...to make ready a people prepared for the Lord." In John God was once again beginning a new exodus event, a new act of salvation which would call the wayward people of God home again. Israel would be led to salvation once more, this time by God dwelling on earth in Jesus.

But it is not until the book of Revelation that we have news of the most astounding ingathering. This will not merely be a gathering of those who are scattered around the earth. This will be a gathering in of those who have left the earth: those imprisoned by the sea and by death and by Hades. It is a gathering up for the new heaven and the new earth where God will dwell with God's faithful people. And again, those who experience this new exodus event will inherit the kingdom, they will be the children of their glorious God, a sign that their God can do glorious things.

We have seen God act for our ancestors at the Red Sea, and we have seen God act for us in Jesus. Our calling then is as clear as the calling of Israel. We are to be a sign to the nations that our God can do wonderful liberating things. Our lives are to proclaim the new and coming exodus, the new heaven and the new earth where mourning and crying, pain and death will be no more, where the healing will finally be done.

Tuesday

A city with the glory of God

Isaiah 28.9–22
Revelation 21.9–21
Luke 1.26–38

In the Spirit he carried me away
to a great high mountain and showed me
the holy city Jerusalem coming down
out of heaven from God. It has the glory of God...
Revelation 21.10,11

The story which is found in the last few chapters of the book of Revelation is in some ways quite unbelievable. Not only will there be a new heaven and a new earth, but the focus of all of it seems to be a new *city*, the new Jerusalem. Cities in our day and age seldom strike us as places of hope. In ancient times, however, cities were considered at least to be places of security. Like all ancient cities, Jerusalem was intended to be a place of refuge and shelter in times of war. And in order to be a secure place in the face of military attack, the city needed to have a solid foundation upon which were built strong walls which could withstand a military siege. Quite literally, the foundations of the city would determine the character of the city, whether it was a secure haven or merely a trap for those within it.

The problem for Isaiah was that the rulers of Jerusalem had built on a foundation of death. The refuge which they sought was in lies and their shelter was in falsehood. Their security was based on deception: they had been deluded into thinking that death would pass them by. They had forgotten their covenant with the living God and had instead made a covenant with death.

But God had not forgotten Jerusalem; God determined to lay the foundation which the rulers had not laid themselves: a precious cornerstone and sure foundation. That stone would be the foundation for walls that were built according to the measure of justice, that were calculated according to the mark set by righteousness. Those of us who are used to reading these lines as descriptions of Jesus, tend to emphasize the character of these verses as words of hope. But for the inhabitants of Jerusalem, who had covenanted with death, this prophecy was a word of condemnation. For when justice and righteousness are the measure, then a city built on lies has no foundation: it will be beaten down and swept away when the crisis comes.

The contrast between the weak and insecure foundation of Jerusalem in Isaiah's time and the solidity of the New Jerusalem in John's vision is stark. Walls of jasper, foundations studded with jewels, gates of pearl—this city is not only strongly built, but beautifully built. Justice and righteousness come to tangible expression with the beautiful stones of the creation.

If so much loving craftsmanship has gone into the building of the city, what sort of refuge and shelter will it be? How will it manifest the righteousness which God envisions for it? Will it be a place where homelessness confronts us, where we encounter shockingly high crime statistics, where slums will be found, where modern office towers raise themselves up to the god of commerce, where breathing will be hazardous to one's health? Or will it be a place where the glory of creation, of humanity and of God will be revealed? Perhaps our cities too clearly reveal the nature of their foundations.

Wednesday

A city for the healing of the nations

Isaiah 29.13–24
Revelation 21.22 – 22.5
Luke 1.39–56

On either side of the river
is the tree of life with its twelve kinds of fruit,
producing its fruit each month,
and the leaves of the trees are for the healing of the nations.
Revelation 22.2

Our God is a God who does amazing and shocking things, not only with cities, but with the people within them (Isa 29.14). As we have been reading through Isaiah this Advent, many of the actions of our God have been actions of judgement; judgement which was incredibly shocking for Jerusalem, the city secure on the holy hill. Our reading today, however, focuses on the redemptive side of that judgement. The people of Isaiah's time had been turning things upside down (v.16) in an evil reversal of creator and creature. God responds with an astounding reversal of God's own, a reversal of blessing: the deaf shall hear, the blind shall see, and the meek and needy people will exult with joy. For the oppressor shall be disinherited and those who manipulate the court system and deny justice shall all be sent away, cast out, cut off. This is precisely the reversal celebrated by Mary: the rich are brought down from thrones (seats of government) and the lowly are lifted (Luke 1.52); the hungry will be fully satisfied with good food and the rich will be sent away empty (1.53). The judgement of God bestows blessing where it is most sorely needed.

The turning of evil into good is quite an astounding thing. But what is perhaps most shocking about these passages is that these reversals are not radically new. They are, quite simply, the tasks to which Israel had been originally called. That is why Jacob (or Israel) will no longer be ashamed when these things come to pass (Isa 29.22). For Israel will finally be fulfilling her task; a task hinted at in both the Isaiah passage and by Mary in Luke. This God, who redeemed Abraham (Isa 29.22), made a promise to him (Luke 1.55) that through his people the nations would be blessed. Through the people of God healing would come to the world. The turning of brokenness into wholeness, injustice into justice was to be the task of the people whom God had called to be God's own.

In light of these passages, then, our text for today takes on an added dimension. The city of God which will provide light for the nations, will also contain a tree, and the leaves of the tree are for the healing of the nations. The whole biblical story, with its specific calling of the people of God, informs this verse: the people of God are the leaves of the trees. We bring the healing. We take on the calling of our saviour, celebrated and awaited this Advent. We are called to fill the hungry with good things, to bring justice where there is manipulation, to see that the ones denied justice are given justice, to lift up the lowly, and to give the meek cause to rejoice. Our role this Advent is to mediate salvation and healing in anticipation of the One who will finally complete the task for us, that we too may no longer be ashamed.

Thursday

A safe and open city

Isaiah 33.13–22
Revelation 22.6–15
Luke 1.57–66

Blessed are those who wash their robes,
so that they will have the right to the tree of life
and may enter the city by the gates.
Revelation 22.14

A couple of days ago we asked what sort of a city would manifest God's justice and righteousness. Yesterday that question was partially answered: a city out of which healing comes, healing for the nations. Today that question is answered in yet another way: the city where God's glory dwells will be a city of security and refuge. It will be a place where the terrors of foreign oppressors—who assess how much money the people should be giving and who count out how many towers there are for fortification—will merely be food for musing thought, not a real danger. The city will be a place where the people are not living in exile among foreigners whose language sounds halting and stammering to the unaccustomed and uncomprehending ear. Moreover, the city will be like a tent which is immovable, which cannot be torn down. This is a different image from that of a city with firm foundation stones, but the thrust is the same. The city will also be fertile, a place with much water. But notice what sort of water is described here: broad and shallow streams where a tall ship cannot go. In the ancient Near East water had an ambiguous character. For those who lived in the desert, water was necessary to provide life and to ensure fertility. A God who could provide water was a powerful God indeed. But water could also be the agent of destruction; the waters of the sea could overwhelm those upon it; then the waters became a source of chaos. A God who could control and defeat the chaotic threat of the deep was stronger yet. Water which is not deep enough to handle a stately ship or even a shallow ship with galley oars will not provide a threat to the people dwelling near it. This is a city that will be both fertile and safe.

But who will inherit this city, who will rest in safety within it? Both of our passages from Isaiah and John answer that question in surprisingly similar ways. Those who walk righteously and despise the gain of oppression, who wave away a bribe and don't want to hear about killing (Isa 33.15)—they will be the ones who look on Jerusalem. Those who have been washed by the blood of the lamb, who have endured the tribulation, who have washed their robes, who do not practice immorality, murder, idolatry or falsehood (Rev 22.15)—they will be the ones who are permitted to enter the city and to share in the inheritance (Rev 21.7).

Throughout the biblical story those who will be welcomed into the city are those who can make that city a place of healing and refuge, rather than a place where injustice and falsehood prevail. The implications provide a challenge to all of us who live in the modern city. If we are not working to walk righteously in our cities, to provide homes for the homeless, food for the hungry, water for the thirsty, and justice for those who are oppressed—in short, if we are not making our cities places of safety and fertile plenty—are we truly preparing for the coming of a saviour who will welcome us into the city by the gates?

Friday

The city of life

Isaiah 35.1 – 10
Revelation 22.16 – 21
Luke 1.67–80

And you, child, will be called the prophet
of the Most High;
for you will go before the Lord to prepare his ways,
to give knowledge of salvation to his people
by forgiveness of their sins.
Luke 1.76,77

As this week has progressed we have looked at various aspects of the new Jerusalem which we await. But we are not a people who dwell in that city; we are still in advent, a pilgrim people, wandering in what seems to be a desert wilderness, journeying toward the city of healing, safety, and the glory of God. What words do the scriptures have for those of us who are undertaking this journey, who desperately want this city but are not yet there?

Today's passage from Isaiah speaks to us in the context of the wilderness; speaks to those of us who feel we are wandering, who don't know how to find the place of healing in the midst of so much brokenness. This is a passage for those of us with weak hands and feeble knees revealing the fear within us (v.3,4). And what is the word which should answer our anxieties? Our God will come with vengeance, with terrible recompense. He will come and save us (v.4)! It seems a puzzling sort of comfort for those of us who associate God's judgement with punishment for our shortfalls. But that is not the emphasis here: the other side of God's judgement is a wonderful salvation which results in healing (v.5,6) and fertility (v.6,7). The dry barrenness of the wilderness will be wet and lush, hot burning sand will become a cool pool of water, ground which is thirsty will be quenched with springs of water, dry desert grass will become succulent reeds and rushes. The barrenness and futility which we experience in our modern lives can blossom for us, says Isaiah; even this place can be a place of healing and refreshment.

But even with the lushness, this is still the wilderness. We can't deny the brokenness which we have created, even when healing begins to happen. This wilderness is not our destination; it is the setting for a highway, a road, a path for the people of God. It will be a safe road, with no place for anything that destroys (v.9), a road that counters the confusion of the wilderness (v.8). Moreover, it will be a road of return, a road which brings us back to the place of our original calling, home to the dwelling place of God, Zion, the new Jerusalem, where singing and joy will cast out sorrow and sadness (v.10).

Zechariah knew about this way. In fact, he knew that his child was called to prepare that way, to make ready a people who would be able to walk that path of salvation. But John would be able to proclaim an aspect of salvation which the prophet Isaiah never even imagined; John would proclaim a healing which was possible because the brokenness was addressed at its most fundamental level—deep within the heart of human beings. The knowledge of salvation that John would proclaim came through the forgiveness of sins (Luke 2.77). It is through this forgiveness that our feet can be guided, said Zechariah, in the ways of peace (v.79). It is through this forgiveness that we too are able to begin to prepare this way, that we are able to experience healing in our barren culture and life-giving plenty in a context of deathly satiation. Because we know that our weak knees are strengthened by the hands of God, that our past failures are forgiven and no longer bind us, we can accept the gift of life-giving water from the Spirit and the Bride and begin to use that water to foster life in the wilderness, en route to the city of life which we await.

Saturday

The city of rest

Isaiah 40.1–11
Matthew 11.28–30

Come to me, all you who are weary
and are carrying heavy burdens,
and I will give you rest.
Matthew 11.28

It has been a long haul. And it continues to be a long haul. Zechariah had to wait to see the prophecies fulfilled. So did the exiles of Isaiah's time. And so do we. For four weeks now we have been waiting. For a whole generation the exiled Israelites had to wait. And for two millennia the church has been waiting. And it is hard. We begin to wonder whether this "coming" will ever be realized. We begin to lose hope. We begin to join the company of the discomforted exiles lulled into believing that things will never really change. The present empire of brokenness, injustice and pain will never end.

And just when we are ready to call it quits the prophet arrives with astounding news. Exile is not the last word! Despair must be dispelled by a word of comfort. "Comfort, O comfort my people, says your God." There will be a homecoming. Zechariah has seen that a way is being prepared in the wilderness. Your exile is over!

But the prophet himself can barely believe it. He is told to prophesy: "Cry out!" And he asks, "What am I to cry?" "The grass withers, the flower fades; but the word of our God will stand forever." Your present reality of exile is not the final word because the empire's days are numbered! These oppressive regimes of injustice and cruelty do not exercise final sovereignty in history, they will necessarily fade and wither. The final sovereignty in history, the only thing that will stand forever, is the word of God.

And what does that word say? It announces a new political reality. The city of Jerusalem—which has been a site of such bad news of judgement throughout much of our Advent readings this year—is now told to take strength, lift up its voice, do not fear, and proclaim the good news: "Here is your God!" It is this word that we have been waiting to hear for four weeks. It is this word that comes to transform our despair into comfort.

And what will this God *do* when he comes? He will rule. Advent is about the coming of the Kingdom. This enthroned God comes with might "and his arm rules for him." But what will be the character of that rule? "He will feed his flock like a shepherd; he will gather the lambs in his arms." His mighty arm will establish his soveriegnty over all of creation and over history. But it will be the loving, caring and nurturing sovereignty that we would expect to find in the protective arms of a shepherd.

We can miss Advent by not being ready, or by simply not waiting because we feel that we have nothing to wait for in our state of arrived self-sufficiency. Even if we know that we have not arrived and we are not self-sufficient; even when we realize that we still live in an empire that scoffs at justice and continues to neglect the poor, abuse the environment, and trust the technologies of war, we still feel incredibly burdened. We feel weighted down, exhausted, powerless and comfortless. To the exiles, Yahweh proclaimed comfort and political redemption. To us Yahweh's Servant says, "Come to me, all you who are weary and are carrying heavy burdens, and I will give you rest." And as we come to him we say, "Amen, come soon Lord Jesus." Maranatha.

The way to the city

Isaiah 52.7–12
Luke 2.1–20

The Lord has bared his holy arm
before the eyes of all the nations;
and all the ends of the earth shall see
the salvation of our God.
Isaiah 52.10

It has happened; the arrival for which we have been waiting is here. "Your God reigns," says the messenger in Isaiah; the kingdom of justice and righteousness we have been reflecting on has finally arrived. But has it, really? The exiles to whom the words of Isaiah 52 were addressed might not have thought so. This message of peace, of the good news of the salvation of their God, came to them deep in the midst of their exile. They had no tangible evidence that their God reigned. There was nothing going on in their situation to suggest that their God had really returned to Zion, had really redeemed this people. But still it was being proclaimed: God is returning to the city; God has redeemed Jerusalem; God has bared God's holy arm; God has arrived to comfort the people! What sort of return and arrival could this be?

An answer is indicated by the text itself, for immediately after this arrival is proclaimed, the people are addressed in language reminiscent of the exodus: "Depart, depart, go out from there!...For you shall not go out in haste, and you shall not go in flight; for the Lord will go before you, and the God of Israel will be your rear guard" (v.11,12). The arrival of God in salvation, it seems, does not mean that all has been accomplished. The redemption of God is only the beginning of something new. The coming of God in history, described as the Lord rolling up his shirt sleeves (v.10), is not a *fait accompli*. It is the beginning of a new exodus event for these exiles, the beginning of a new trek through the wilderness towards the city of God. The return of the Lord to Zion is the return of a God who is leading a people through the wilderness, guiding them by day and by night.

The baring of God's arm in Jesus, the coming of God in history, proclaims exactly this sort of beginning. "Glory to

God in the highest heaven, and on earth peace among those whom he favours!" proclaim the angel messengers. The Israelites in first-century Palestine had no evidence that peace had come upon the earth; the people of God in the twentieth century have no evidence of this peace either. Can we say that our God has really arrived and brought salvation? Well, the story of the birth of Jesus is only the beginning of the gospel, the start of the story of good news. The coming of God in Jesus is the beginning of a path that leads to the death and resurrection of God's very self.

In Isaiah the return of God leads to a new exodus and then, inexorably, the prophet moves into the song of the suffering servant of Isaiah 53. This is no quick fix, no easy solution. The salvation of God begins in a stable and reaches its climax on a cross. The new life, the healing of which we have spoken, is a resurrection life, a resurrection healing that can come only through the agony of death.

Today's celebration is a celebration then, not only of an arrival, but also of a beginning; the beginning of our God coming to dwell with us, coming to lead us on our own exodus journey through the wilderness. And in this coming, God has become one of us, become human, and has invited us to become like the true human Jesus. But we must remember that this is a new beginning in the middle of the story; Christmas is not the end of our waiting, nor of the tale that we tell. We still carry the vision of Isaiah and of John, a vision of a city of justice and righteousness and life, whose trees are for the healing of the nations. And so today, as we celebrate the coming of our God for salvation, we too set our faces toward Jerusalem, the holy city, knowing that our path also will be through the barrenness of the wilderness before we reach the water of life.

Made in the USA
Monee, IL
25 November 2019

17413117R00039